Sunshine BlackRose

Publications

A Withered Rose Still Blooms

NIMA SHININGSTAR-EL

South Carolina

Copyright © 2019 by Nima Shiningstar-EL.

Published By Sunshine BlackRose Publications
P. O. Box 1283
Clearwater, SC 29822
www.sunshinebrpublications.com

All rights reserved. Printed in the United States of America. No part of this book may be used or reproduced in any manner whatsoever without written permission except in the case of brief quotations em- bodied in critical articles or reviews.

Book and Cover design by Sunshine BlackRose Publications

ISBN: 978-1732191037

1732191037

Dedication

This book is dedicated out of love to every man, woman, and child that has experienced Domestic Violence. To each individual that suffers from PTSD due to Domestic Violence. To every survivor and to those that have unfortunately lost their lives due to it. From the 911 calls that were answered too late...to the person that said they would not go back and did but never made it out again...To that someone that thought that love came from a busted lip or a black eye...from those that watched their parents go through this tragedy and learned that this was their normal...to the child that can't speak up for themselves...This book is for you.

I was that little girl in the closet hiding while my father hit my mother
I was that woman who was hit while she was pregnant
I was so many different people at different times in my life
I am also a survivor and if you are reading this...so are you!

The Build·UP

Every step I take seems like a time bomb about to explode.
I can feel the tension in the air.
The heavy breathing•••
How everything annoys them and now tiptoe is the normal walk.
The music is too loud.
Everything you do is wrong.
Waiting around for what is to come next.
You make more and more mistakes in their eyes and you try to disappear into the walls.
You somewhat become a silent partner waiting for the bridge to collapse.

A Withered Rose Still Blooms

Nima Shiningstar-El

A Withered Rose Still Blooms

NIMA SHININGSTAR-EL

If you or someone you know is experiencing Domestic Violence please safely call The Domestic Violence Hotline at 1-866-723-3014

A Withered Rose Still Blooms

A Withered Rose Still Blooms

Nima Shiningstar-El

You are a survivor

You can move on to bigger and better things

Look at yourself in the mirror and remind yourself that life can be a challenge.

That it may be a struggle and though you may fall over and over...You will still stand tall

If you or someone you know is experiencing Domestic Violence please safely call The Domestic Violence Hotline at

1-866-723-3014

The Honeymoon

This is normally the time after abuse has taken place. Now you may get flowers, cards, candy, and love notes around the house for no reason.

He or she is so polite and in love. They are regretful and remorseful. They remember all the little things that they did to get you in the first place. It seems as if the romance is back. You let down your guard and think that everything is ok and that they are never going to go down that dark road again. All of the promises flow and you are floating but you have been down this road before.

When will I learn? I fell in love. I wanted love and injuries and insults is all I have now. I still feel as if there is good deep down. I just have to find it.

Nima Shiningstar-El

When children experience domestic violence in the home they are sometimes more in danger of becoming an abusive adult or being abused.

We must break the cycle

There is a way but as with anything, you must admit that you a problem.

If you are willing to take that first major step, you are almost there.

Never give up the fight.

Women and men alike are Abusers and Victims….

Provokers and Survivors

We must reach higher and higher

If you or someone you know is experiencing Domestic Violence please safely call The Domestic Violence Hotline at

1-866-723-3014

A Withered Rose Still Blooms

>Because he touched her way too soon
>Because he learned that women were objects
>Because she thought she had to hit first
>Because they both thought love was at the end of a fist
>They two took turns hurting one another

Nima Shiningstar-El

Just tell me what it is and I will fix it...1 hope

No need for harsh words or cuts to the emotions

The words hurt enough

I cry in the dark begging for light

I would never want to make you cry

If you cry then we both cry and that's too many tears between us

If you or someone you know is experiencing Domestic Violence please safely call The

Domestic Violence Hotline at

1-866-723-3014

A Withered Rose Still Blooms

> I walked away because my life depended on it
> That sun grew dark and I prayed for light
> Prayed for love at one time
> But I was not ready and so it hid until I was
> Tried to keep him with sex...Wrong
> Tried to cook my way to him...wrong
> Tried to be what he wanted me to be and that was wrong...
> I had no wrong left and he still beat me
> I walked away before love killed me

Nima Shiningstar-El

Remembering a time when I could speak up without worrying about being slapped or dragged through the house.

No one wanted to help.

No one seemed to care,

I thought that I would be dead at a very young age

Yet here I am telling my story

I am a survivor!!!

I used to think of myself as a victim….

NEVER AGAIN

If you or someone you know is experiencing Domestic Violence please safely call The

Domestic Violence Hotline at

1-866-723-3014

A Withered Rose Still Blooms

Imagine being able to come into a safe home.
Food cooking and beautiful floral smells.
Children waiting to run into your arms.
I always thought that my home would be filled with love because that's the way I grew up.
I prayed that one day I could come into a home with all the things I love.
I have been trapped in this loveless marriage.
At some point I thought we loved one another but only to come to the realization that he wanted to control me.
Can you believe that at some point I actually thought this was love and couldn't see anything else?
He isolated me from my family and worked daily on diminishing my self-esteem.

Nima Shiningstar-El

They didn't know she held on to that betrayal and could not allow it to die.
Every other second was filled with hurt and regret
It became somehow her cover Hard to shake
Meant for it to melt
Wanted the thoughts to exit her emotions
Hated that it somehow and some way consumed her
It hurt... thought she felt love as it tiptoe around her heart but it was just for pleasure sake
How far did they really go?
How far would they have gone?
How that smile for so long covered his secret and she allowed him to continue to rest his so called loving words in her ear
She sipped his fake emotions like a fine wine and poured her false approval over the meal
It was her honor amongst what they have since become...
In a Matrimony of deception

If you or someone you know is experiencing Domestic Violence please safely call The Domestic Violence Hotline at

1-866-723-3014

A Withered Rose Still Blooms

Heard about women abusing men but never thought it would be me

Big Strong me

Loving Me

Father and Faithful me

Thought he loved me

Love doesn't feel this way

Yet words love keep coming from his lips

Love doesn't feel bad

No longer want this type of love

Thought love was what we had

We had nothing

I want nothing more

Nima Shiningstar-El

I thought I knew what love was

All I wanted to do was leave my mother's home

From that house to a house of hell

Too afraid to tell anyone what I was going through

My husband beat me bad

I tried to run and my family convinced me to go back to him

That he loved me

That it wasn't as bad as I made it out to be

That he was my husband

My children loved him

He is a great provider

They can't hear me cry at night

Why should I be sad as long as my children are happy?

But are they?

If you or someone you know is experiencing Domestic Violence please safely call The Domestic Violence Hotline at

1-866-723-3014

A Withered Rose Still Blooms

Nima Shiningstar-El

If you or someone you know is experiencing Domestic Violence please safely call The

Domestic Violence Hotline at

1-866-723-3014

A Withered Rose Still Blooms

Nima Shiningstar-El

It's not in me to leave you
I'm sitting and wondering why so many women are attracted to you
Maybe it's because they don't know what you do to me
They have no clue that you will hurt them in the end
They have no idea how often I cry
No need to lie
All the smiles and bullshit
Why can't I walk away?

If you or someone you know is experiencing Domestic Violence please safely call The

Domestic Violence Hotline at

1-866-723-3014

A Withered Rose Still Blooms

All of the sweet things you said to me
Had me bragging to my friends about you
The candles
The trips
The Black eye
The busted lip
The car
The house
A cheating spouse
The money
The jewels
You broke my ribs
Then broke the rules
This smile
So fake
I want to break
Killing me slow and hard while the world wishes they were us

Nima Shiningstar-El

The First Time

I remember dreaming of my first time

I was afraid but ready

My girlfriends warned me that it would hurt

After that I would be a woman

My curves would come out a little more

My breasts would actually be what they are supposed to be

My first time would be special and exciting

My body would crave him and I would forever be his angel

My first time...

I was pushed to the ground

Did not make a sound

Except for the sound of silence

Silence...that cold icy silence

The kind that sits in your throat and marinates and gathers all of

your fears, all of you insecurities

All of your doubts and begs intrusion to stop

My first time I learned the hard way to give a blow job... that came

with a few hard slaps and some simple hair pulling

What was I doing?

If you or someone you know is experiencing Domestic Violence please safely call The

Domestic Violence Hotline at

1-866-723-3014

A Withered Rose Still Blooms

Why was I here?

But he loved me and since I had nothing to compare it to I thought

that as long as he was my husband

As long as he paid the bills and as long as I was the little housewife

it was ok

I made it ok for him to do whatever, whenever, he decided to do it

and I did nothing

One day I did more than nothing

And I don't want you to wait to do more than nothing and end up

doing more than something

Do nothing now

Do something now

LEAVE

Because the first time may be your last time.

Nima Shiningstar-El

She Never Knew

She never knew what true love was.
They only wanted her body...
So over developed and so under aged.
She never knew what true happiness in a relationship was about
Saw what she wanted to see until she could see no more
What was this thing called love that some seem to have gotten from its hiding place
How she wished and hoped never finding it

If you or someone you know is experiencing Domestic Violence please safely call The Domestic Violence Hotline at

1-866-723-3014

How?

How can this be love?

I thought love was beautiful and bright

Pretty colors and hard work

How can this loud and scary place be love?

Thought love was tender and gentle?

Not hard and jagged!

It has pricked me and made me bleed

The bandage is too small and the hurt soaks through

Through yells and clinched fists

Through salted tears I pray

Maybe tomorrow will be the day?

Maybe he will not kill me?

Maybe he won't let the children hear today?

Maybe he will beat me in silence?

Maybe he will grow tired?

Maybe he will realize that there are no more free spaces on my arms

for him to bruise?

MAYBE?

Nima Shiningstar-El

NO MORE

My arms are no longer yours to grab and pull!

My eyes are not your targets!

That gun looks so inviting I can see it out of the corner of my eyes

Remember you showed me how to aim higher than your target

Why would you teach me that?

Is it your secret desire to die at the hands of me?

Is guilt your lover?

Somehow that cold heart can feel?

That black gun...

Looks sexy

Violence that will end violence

Yet all I want to do is be free

Free to live life without regret

This stomach is off limits as your personal punching bag

No more will I hide my face with my hands to shield myself

Yes I am afraid...but I fear what may come next if I do not say...

NO MORE!

If you or someone you know is experiencing Domestic Violence please safely call The Domestic Violence Hotline at

1-866-723-3014

A Withered Rose Still Blooms

She laid in his arms and pretended not to know his lies
Lies that have long crushed her beneath his layers
Holding on to the girl-ish smile
How well they have mastered this dance
Lovingly he kissed her and saw the desire for others
They both lay in waiting for the right moment
The moment to speak truth into the air
What becomes of former lovers?
Do they simply fade into the night as the sunset or do they linger as
ice to naked branches in winter fall?
Cold as the next touch that pretend to be genuine though they are

Nima Shiningstar-El

She never thought she was pretty
Counted her flaws and divided them by two
Mirrors became her enemy
How could anyone love her like this?
The way she needed to be loved
Is love that elusive?
Is she not worthy?
At night she cries
During the day she is a force
Heartache puts her to sleep
Pain covers her like a perfectly fitted quilt
Moisture from her tears are her comfort
In the dark she can cry as loud and as hard as she needs to
No one comes between her tears and her cheeks
This is the way she has learned to speak

If you or someone you know is experiencing Domestic Violence please safely call The Domestic Violence Hotline at

1-866-723-3014

What if?

What if you truly loved me?
What if I actually made you happy?
What if we loved one another the way outsiders believe?
What if she never existed...though I understand that she made you hate me or maybe that was already your truth?
What if he never comforted me?
What if he hadn't kissed my tears away?
What if I didn't dream of killing you each night?
What if you didn't beat me?
What if my pain came from someone else other than you?
What if our wedding vows meant something to us?

Nima Shiningstar-El

Where were you

I yelled and no one came to my rescue

I ran and you watched as he chased me down

I screamed and you ignored my voice

You helped to take my voice away

He chased me and grabbed me

He choked me and slapped me

He called me all types of names and you and your friends laughed

You recorded it

You downloaded it

You shared it and talked about the way I should have ran after he

turned his head to make sure no one was looking

It got over a million likes and no one said a thing

Where were you?

If you or someone you know is experiencing Domestic Violence please safely call The

Domestic Violence Hotline at

1-866-723-3014

A Withered Rose Still Blooms

It was completely and without remorse that he took what he wanted
and didn't care to hear my cries
Originally felt safe with him
He became my protector
Something so innocent turned into my nightmare
Lives shattered that sunrise
Never to look at another sunrise the same
My heart sank to an endless pit
Yelling from a well that went too deep for those that claimed they
loved me
To find vultures circled my lifeless body as I try to remember where
I was and where I belonged
Was I even human any longer?
That dead look in my eyes I was afraid to see me
Stretched out my hands just hoping that someone would grab
hold....no one did
And so here I lay... dying
Walking around
Waiting to hurt
Just as I was hurt
Pain brings pain
I died inside a long time ago

Nima Shiningstar-El

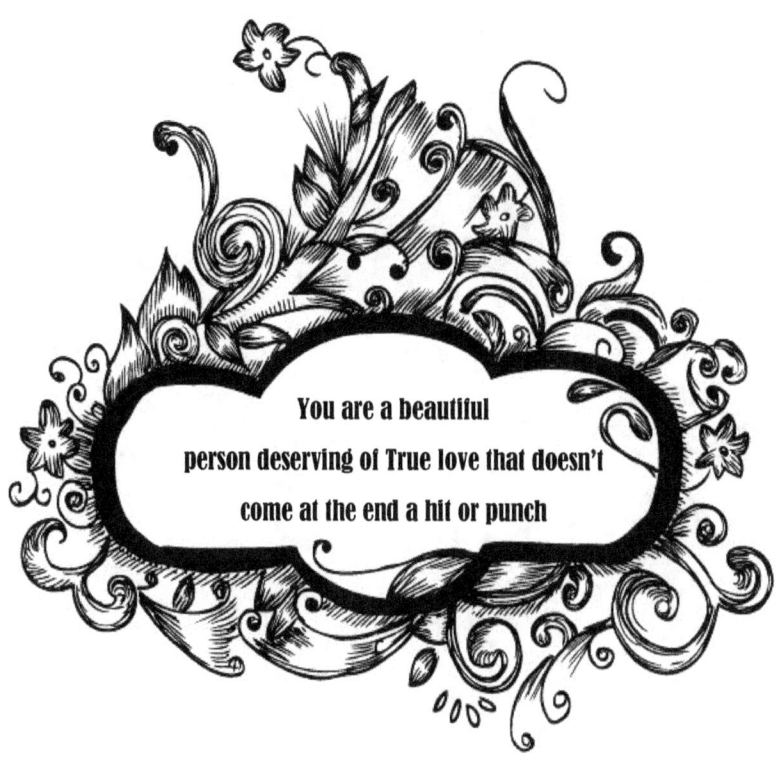

If you or someone you know is experiencing Domestic Violence please safely call The Domestic Violence Hotline at

1-866-723-3014

A Withered Rose Still Blooms

Nima Shiningstar-El

Monsters In Your Room

One kiss sealed my fate

That was so impressive of you

You took my life in the one move

Did you finally find the monsters under the bed?

This was always the excuse for your abuse

If you or someone you know is experiencing Domestic Violence please safely call The Domestic Violence Hotline at

1-866-723-3014

Your So called Love

I loved you once before but you beat that love into a black hole
How is love this hard?
Why are the colors of your love Black and Blue?
I tried to be all that I thought you wanted me to be but I was still not good enough
You made me forget that I was a Queen!
How could I forget that I was a Queen?

Nima Shiningstar-El

Bruises across my lips
I hide in the corner waiting on the next move
My side hurts from kicks that you gave me
I tried to be a good husband but you have beat it out of me
I want this pain to go away
I will not lay down and die
Survival is in my spirit
Though you hurt me
I will still pray for you

If you or someone you know is experiencing Domestic Violence please safely call The Domestic Violence Hotline at

1-866-723-3014

A Withered Rose Still Blooms

I look in the mirror every day and there is not one day
That goes by that I don't see your hands over my mouth

Feel your fingers between my legs

Not a day goes by that I don't feel afraid that you will come back to get me

You have been long gone
But you have broken my trust for the rest of my days
I must learn to live without the fear of you
You stole my innocence
Stole my younger years
Why was this your goal?
Was I your original target?
Why did they ignore my cries?
Why did they believe your lies?

Nima Shiningstar-El

I left a long time ago
She never noticed though
The first hit shocked and surprised me
It was followed by things I couldn't believe
Nights waking in cold sweats
Christmas' that should have been merry now too horrible to forget
My friends laughed when I told them what was taking place
Until the realized the serious look on my face
Yes, my wife beat me and just because I am a big man
Solving my marital problems with violence was never in the plan
Yet mentally and physically broken….
Here I stand

If you or someone you know is experiencing Domestic Violence please safely call The Domestic Violence Hotline at

1-866-723-3014

Dark Lover

The dark is my lover
It holds me and hides me from those eyes that look to destroy me
I have learned to make love to the dark
So that it would shield me from his grip
I love you darkness
Please don't lead me into the light and make cold hands aware of me
I hear footsteps but they stumble and fumble unable to catch the prey
So he calls out to me like a master to a slave
To come and tie myself to the whipping post
The dark is my friend
The dark is my friend
The dark is my lover

Nima Shiningstar-El

Never meant to hurt you

Tell me how not to?

Missed out on love

Thought I knew with you?

You made it easy

I always seem to make it hard

No more raised fist to your beautiful face

I will shout no more

Help is near

I feel it when I pray

I pray that we can both walk away unharmed

Signed,

Your Abuser

If you or someone you know is experiencing Domestic Violence please safely call The Domestic Violence Hotline at

1-866-723-3014

A Withered Rose Still Blooms

My story may not be your story yet we share a special bond
Hands around my throat
Try not to choke
Thought sex would save me
Beatings to my body and spirit is what she gave me
Stopped dating men long ago because I knew that a woman would
understand
I never wanted to be with another man
Thought because we share the same things
That abuse would no longer be a thing
I was so wrong
I allowed it to go on for so long

Nima Shiningstar-El

It started with the word Bitch
I felt so low
My life changed for the worse
Made to feel as if I was not important
Made to feel less of a Queen
I am not a Bitch
I AM A QUEEN

If you or someone you know is experiencing Domestic Violence please safely call The Domestic Violence Hotline at

1-866-723-3014

A Withered Rose Still Blooms

Mommy and daddy fight a lot but I am use to it

Kicks and hits

Blood from both of their lips

So now I know what to do when I grow up and find a wife

This is just a part of life

Right?

Signed...Someone's child

A Withered Rose Still Blooms

Nima Shiningstar-El

Hey You!

You are halfway through the book!

Have you read enough?

Have you made a decision?

Do you need to go through any more pain?

Will you get help?

If not for you then what about your sons and daughters?

Do they deserve to see you like this?

Do they deserve to be next?

If you or someone you know is experiencing Domestic Violence please safely call The Domestic Violence Hotline at

1-866-723-3014

A Withered Rose Still Blooms

Poor Little girl she so sad.
Once was a good little girl now all she is ....is bad
You know they say her momma left her on the church steps when she was a baby...her momma was a crazy lady
Her daddy well...that's another story

Those eyes so sad always wishing for what she never had
Too damn bad
Starving for attention and always from the wrong folks
Don't she know her uncle is a pervert?
Her auntie sat back and watched all of that

You know she too big to be sittin on her uncle's lap
At least not like that
No one cared until her belly grew

No one seemed to care until folks starting asking...who?
Who baby you carry in your belly?
Come on now child...tell me?
Who touched you baby?
I swear I will kill him where he stand
You too young to be had by some man
So late that night
While the moon was bright
She walked as far from the house in order to be out of sight

Had that baby in the field of cotton where there was blood from farm owners crackin whips over black backs
Cried to GOD while she covered her mouth as that new life ripped her
Now sweat poured from her face and blood ran down her legs
Crawled back to the house with the cord still in place
Standing in the door was granny with tears covering her face
Took those babies in her arms
Cut the cord...said a prayer, fed them, and tucked them in bed

Nima Shiningstar-El

Hitting you makes me feel powerful
It fuels my fire
I love to know that you are in pain
Can you tell me why that is?
It seems as if I step outside of my body and someone else takes over
I tried to pray it away
Tried to push it out of my mind
I can't...so now what?

If you or someone you know is experiencing Domestic Violence please safely call The Domestic Violence Hotline at

1-866-723-3014

A Withered Rose Still Blooms

Stop!

I know you are scared

I was too

I know you think that you have no one who cares...

I care

It's hard

It's dark and cold

The sun will shine again

You can make it

If you go back you may never get another chance to leave

Think about it?

Nima Shiningstar-El

You made me silent

My voice was no longer important

How can I be to blame for this?

My innocence was stripped away and I became a prisoner in my own body

Covering every inch of skin that showed

Never allowed to explore my sexuality because you ripped it from me

That was my right

To become a woman

Once thought of as a flower and now weeds are what they see and you were the cause of it

I wanted to say this to you for some time and I had to write it down because I am still afraid of you

If you or someone you know is experiencing Domestic Violence please safely call The Domestic Violence Hotline at 1-866-723-3014

A Withered Rose Still Blooms

I never meant to hit
I gave up on me long ago
So I gave up on you too
Never knew what love was
So how could I give it to you?
My father ran away
Mother did too
Little girl lost
Bruises black and blue
Learned that it was ok to lash out
Scream and shout
Resolving issues were not what this family was about
So please walk away
Before I hurt you again
Breakings bonds that we can't mend

Nima Shiningstar-El

I realize that you never truly loved me or maybe you just never knew me
How are we still at this point, in the hell of it?
I know that you love her
I see through all the pleasant bullshit but this is where we are
At this unspoken place this unspoken space.
How is it possible?
Please tell me to my face

I pulled back the curtain on some of my whispers and I feel that I have jumped too soon
Funny thing is
This feeling is all brand new
Never felt this way before
Afraid of what is in store

Can you tell me that my feelings make no sense?
How those deeds so wrapped in silk and satin turn sour with spit
This funny type shit
I just don't get it

If you or someone you know is experiencing Domestic Violence please safely call The Domestic Violence Hotline at
1-866-723-3014

A Withered Rose Still Blooms

We sit and chat and chit
Please help me if you can understand this
My heart is being tested
I thought we both were invested

Continuing to search for the words or language to fill in the blanks...
You wasted my time with fake lines...
So thanks
I know...
Nobody is perfect but all that side shit you got going on...
And here I thought that you thought that I was worth it...
I know I ain't perfect
I... still... don't... deserve... this

Nima Shiningstar-El

So I can't cry?

I must man up...That's what they call it
No tears allowed?
I want to yell out loud!
Stop putting your hands on me!
I am not your beating post!
Nor am I your target!
Once love blessed us now you have taken that and cursed it
Every name in the book you have called me
As if I don't have feelings
This is hard for me to deal with
Each night afraid to walk through my own house
Every other day you threatening to put me out
Taking my children away and leaving with nothing
All that we have we both built from nothing
We celebrated once we had something
Bruises that I hide from my family
I still can't believe that this is happening to me

If you or someone you know is experiencing Domestic Violence please safely call The Domestic Violence Hotline at 1-866-723-3014

A Withered Rose Still Blooms

Ears to wall
Listening to screams of pain
Afraid for her
She needs help
This happens every weekend
Why doesn't she just leave him?
This is too much
Then I hear them make up and she is yelling but in a different way
She is enjoying his pleasure
Or is it still pain?

Nima Shiningstar-El

For so long I doubted me
No more
Believing in me has been the best thing
I realized that I don't have the issue ...you do
Maybe a lack of love in life prior to me
No one showed you how or gave you an example of love
I am truly sorry for you
I did nothing but try to love you
To be an example for you
I will not allow it to kill me
I am saving my own life

If you or someone you know is experiencing Domestic Violence please safely call The Domestic Violence Hotline at

1-866-723-3014

A Withered Rose Still Blooms

Save Me

The cops couldn't save me
The church couldn't save me
My parents couldn't save me
My friends couldn't save me
Your reach was too far for them
I saved Me

Nima Shiningstar-El

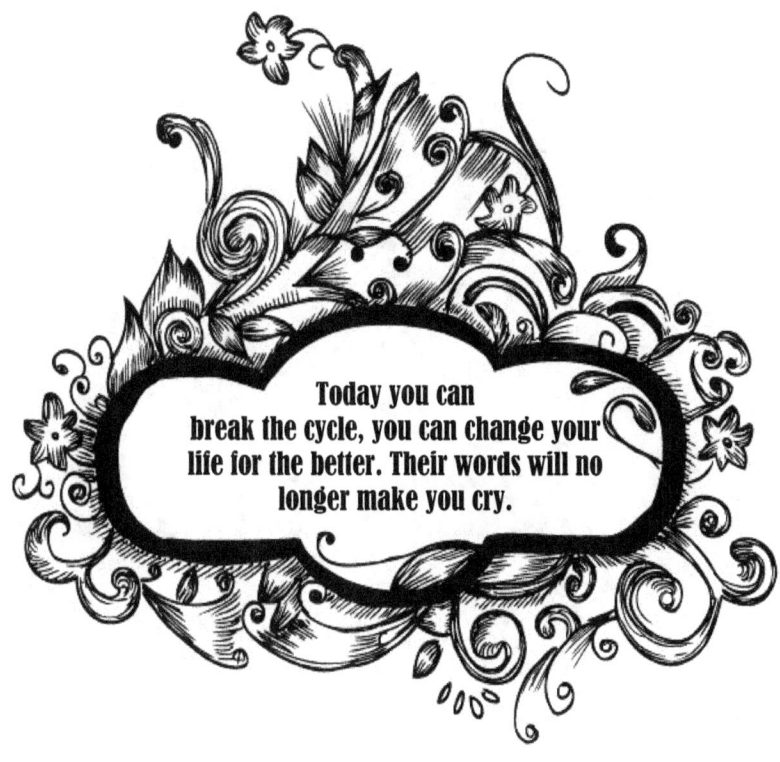

If you or someone you know is experiencing Domestic Violence please safely call The

Domestic Violence Hotline at

1-866-723-3014

A Withered Rose Still Blooms

Nima Shiningstar-El

Today

Today I can breathe again
You are no longer in my life
I no longer have to hide in my closet
And pray you are too drunk to find me

If you or someone you know is experiencing Domestic Violence please safely call The Domestic Violence Hotline at

1-866-723-3014

Choosing Me

I woke up and chose me
I chose to say "NO MORE"
I chose to walk away from pain and hurt
From fear and sorrow
Decided to take a chance on life
A better life
Without you in it
I am a survivor!

Nima Shiningstar-El

I will not die!

Though you may want me to

You can beat my skin and spit in my face

But I will still continue to fly

I know that I am not the only one

We are the unfortunate many

We will strive and move forward

You have tried to kill my spirit and it is too strong

My cry was loud but my strength pulled me through

Now look at you?

You who gave fake love

Controlled me for some time

Now it's my time to shine

And I am Bright

Blinding your negative hands and negative words

Fuck what you thought you heard

Not this Girl!!

Not... this... Girl!

If you or someone you know is experiencing Domestic Violence please safely call The Domestic Violence Hotline at

1-866-723-3014

A Withered Rose Still Blooms

Peace at night now that I have had enough
I never thought that I would be free of you
I sleep sound
I can breathe again
You have no more hold on me
How could this be?
Because I am finally free

Nima Shiningstar-El

Butterfly…

Where is your destination?

Away from here

Is all that I can say for now

The fire is too hot

And my wings were almost destroyed

Butterfly…

Why don't you stay?

Life has become too heavy for me

And I must make my escape

If you or someone you know is experiencing Domestic Violence please safely call The

Domestic Violence Hotline at

1-866-723-3014

A Withered Rose Still Blooms

Broken yet alive

Didn't see it coming

Now I see clearly!

Felt helpless…

Now Strong!

Thought death was the only way out

Life now excites me!

No more hiding in the shadows

Sunlight hits my face and now I long to be free

I am free

Nima Shiningstar-El

My worth

You are not allowed to hit me!

Roses will not make it all better

You are not allowed to kick me!

Telling me that you love me is a lie!

Candy and cards will not mend this broken heart

There are not enough letters in this lifetime to make me stay!

I am beautiful!

I am strong!

You made me think that I was ugly!

How dare you!

I left my faith in me for a minute too long and that is where I went

wrong

Forgot just how strong I was

Never again!

I remember MY WORTH

If you or someone you know is experiencing Domestic Violence please safely call The Domestic Violence Hotline at

1-866-723-3014

A Withered Rose Still Blooms

When I cried you turned your back on me
Made me to feel ashamed of telling the truth
You always told me to tell the truth
I guess the truth was good as long as my truth didn't hurt you and your life.
Why was my young life not worth protecting?
Despite your attempts
I am still standing
Still strong
Still chasing my dreams
I find my smile from time to time
And deep down my laughter erupted often
Despite you and your efforts
I can still love
I still laugh

Nima Shiningstar-El

They will see no more

The hurt

The pain

The tears by your words or hands

I will shield them from your ways until or unless love is at the forefront

This is not their fight

There should be no fight

Yet here we are fighting

Not out loud anymore

If you or someone you know is experiencing Domestic Violence please safely call The Domestic Violence Hotline at
1-866-723-3014

A Withered Rose Still Blooms

I have escaped the hands of you and risen to great expectations
How dare you think that you will continue to crush my spirit?
Look at me
I am beautiful
I am creative
I am GOD's child
Not to be walked upon
You made the mistake of underestimating me
I will shine

Nima Shiningstar-El

I WILL MAKE IT THROUGH
I WILL NOT BE A VICTIM
I AM A SURVIVOR
I LOVE MYSELF
I AM WORTHY

I AM WORTH IT

I LOVE WHO I SEE IN THE MIRROR

If you or someone you know is experiencing Domestic Violence please safely call The Domestic Violence Hotline at

1-866-723-3014

A Withered Rose Still Blooms

Nima Shiningstar-El

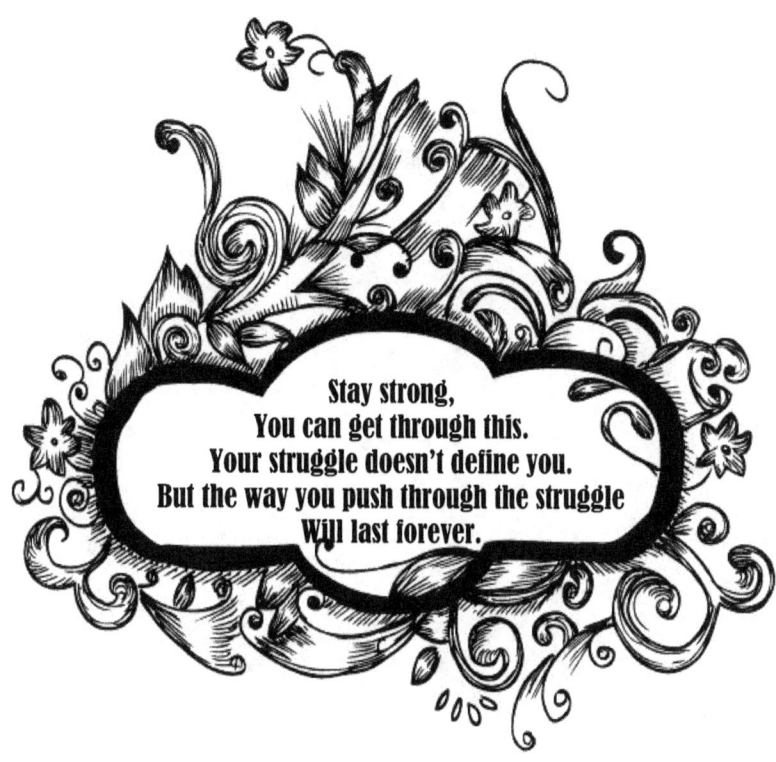

If you or someone you know is experiencing Domestic Violence please safely call The

Domestic Violence Hotline at

1-866-723-3014

A Withered Rose Still Blooms

Nima Shiningstar-El

I was here for a spell and somewhere along the line we created a doorway spiraling into the galaxy knocking over stars and disrespecting the universe

It hurts

My emotions are no longer yours to keep

Continuously filled with anxiety in regards to every word I speak
Are we truly in love or are we just playing this game?

So beautiful is the disguise that hide your lies...covered in flowers and twisted elegance

Entangled and engulfed even entrenched in what seems to be the perfect sunset
Yet we forget and regret that we are on the other side of the moon and burned too soon

The death of Bride and Groom

If you or someone you know is experiencing Domestic Violence please safely call The Domestic Violence Hotline at

1-866-723-3014

A Withered Rose Still Blooms

They say tell your truth
Be transparent
They want to know what my layers look like once they are peeled back
Afraid of myself
I held myself in sheer horror
Unaware that I am still visible to all
They wish me to fall

Nima Shiningstar-El

I once was you

I see right through you I use to be you

In fear of it all

Afraid to call out for help

I was you

Counting scars

Counting the number of hits

The times they missed

How often I bit my nails

Or had busted lips

Fell to my knees because I thought the abuse would stop

Only to have my clothes ripped off as they climbed on top

Smacks to my face as my skin turned hot

Somehow I thought I deserved everything that I got

I didn't love myself because they told me not to

Patches of hair missing, didn't know what to do

She told me she loved me

He said that he cared

Had me afraid and scared

My own shadow made me jump

If you or someone you know is experiencing Domestic Violence please safely call The Domestic Violence Hotline at

1-866-723-3014

A Withered Rose Still Blooms

Afraid of things in the daylight that went bump
Because I somehow was the reason for it all going wrong
Found myself singing the same old song
♪♫"I'm leaving and I ain't coming back to this life" ♪♫
To be grabbed and pushed to the ground with them over top of me
screaming, "You're my wife"
If you leave me I will kill myself
That's when it hit me that we both needed serious help
But I can only take care of myself

Nima Shiningstar-El

To you...

The one that said nothing out of fear and lived with it until now

To you...

The one that told your truth to those that did not listen

To the little girl or boy that hid in the closet and couldn't make friends

because they were too afraid

To the voice that was never heard

To the survivor

To the fighter

To the man that kept his mouth closed because men don't tell

To the person living with PTSD

Living with Nightmares

For the generational curse that has to be broken

You do have a voice

Someone will listen

If you or someone you know is experiencing Domestic Violence please safely call The Domestic Violence Hotline at

1-866-723-3014

A Withered Rose Still Blooms

>Don't be ashamed...you didn't deserve that pain
Tears will fall but you made it through the rain
Every step is forward movement
We all need some self-improvement
This is the day that you move closer towards your destination
Escaping was a part of your destination
Picking up the pieces will be a challenge and sometimes hard
Action with Prayer to the Highest GOD

Nima Shiningstar-El

There she is!
That beautiful person that I once knew
Been gone for too long and for a moment I believed the lies
The lies that told me no one else would ever love me
That no one would care about me
The lie that made me believe that I was ugly...useless...stupid
Every name to make me feel less than a human being
One day I stopped believing the lies and realized just how beautiful I am
How smart I am
Don't believe the lies

Don't believe the lies

If you or someone you know is experiencing Domestic Violence please safely call The Domestic Violence Hotline at
1-866-723-3014

Moving forward

The day I decided to leave was one of the scariest days of my life.
I realized that I could live or die in that very moment.
What if they decided to kill me?
What if they followed me and began to threaten my family and friends?
What if I can't make it financially on my own?

These are very real questions.
But constantly thinking what if... will keep you in a dangerous situation.
What if you can make it financially on your own?
What if they don't come after you?
What if you find someone to treat you the way that you want and need to be treated?
What if you could share your experience with someone and help them to escape domestic Violence?

YOU ARE A SURVIVOR
NO MORE WHAT IF'S

Nima Shiningstar-El

The New Life

Sometimes I wake up in the middle of the night in a cold sweat. I even look over my shoulders and assume that they are following me. Going to the market, taking my child to school. You never really think that it's over. You watch the news and see acts of Domestic Violence and how the abuser will come to hurt or kill you and anyone around you that may stand in the way.

But you know that you can never go back. You are better off as well as your child or children. You wonder how you got into that situation in the first place, but you still move on. You do it because you deserve better. Because your children deserve better. So that others will not go down this path and that your strength will pull up another from their personal hell. Today I am independent, strong, living, I went back to school. Through all of that pain I am still able to laugh hard and true. Able to love and receive love. I don't have nightmares about the abuse any longer and I don't look over my shoulders for that reason. I am a caretaker of people and that's what I love.
Every day is a new day and I look forward to it

Signed a former victim now...A Survivor

If you or someone you know is experiencing Domestic Violence please safely call The Domestic Violence Hotline at
1-866-723-3014

A Withered Rose Still Blooms

Each time the wind blows

I thank the Heavens that I am still alive

I survived

To live

To sing again

To tell my story to those that share similar experiences

And to remind us all that we made it through the storm

I never thought that I would see my smile again and look...

There it is

Nima Shiningstar-El

This has been a battle
I gave up on me long ago
Bare my soul
Left it behind

Then realized that I was not dead
I must move forward
I am too alive to stay still
Tell them I was not defeated
I am that rose that will see light again
You will have no choice but to see me
I am that withered rose that you left behind
Now in full bloom

If you or someone you know is experiencing Domestic Violence please safely call The Domestic Violence Hotline at

1-866-723-3014

A Withered Rose Still Blooms

I was raped by my first husband

I was thrown to the floor when I was 8 months pregnant with my first child

I was hit more than once by my boyfriend as a teenager

All of this was wrong and I said nothing until I was out of these relationships.

Two different men

Two different relationships

And both times it was wrong

I said enough... no more... it's over

I am still standing

I am still blooming

Love Nima

Nima Shiningstar-El

STILL BLOOM

If you or someone you know is experiencing Domestic Violence please safely call The Domestic Violence Hotline at
1-866-723-3014

A Withered Rose Still Blooms

Nima Shiningstar-El

What is safety Planning as it pertains to Domestic Violence?

Safety Planning is a plan of action set in place for the specific reason of fleeing a dangerous situation.
Have a bag packed with important documentation such as all birth certificates, cash, clothes, social security cards, school ID, medical/insurance card, etc.
This bag should be hidden in a location out of sight of your abuser. It can be kept at a friend's or family member's home, a gym, or school locker.

Please speak to a counselor or someone that you can trust, that can help you in your process of breaking away.

Don't forget to call the hotline number for domestic Violence @ 1-866-723-3014 and speak to a hotline counselor

*Credit cards leave a paper trail

If you or someone you know is experiencing Domestic Violence please safely call The Domestic Violence Hotline at
1-866-723-3014

A Withered Rose Still Blooms

Acknowledgments

Thank You...

To all of you that have supported me in any way possible. I appreciate you to the fullest. Your love, friendship, time, energy, presence, and hard work means a great deal to me. From my spirit I say...Thank You

A special thanks goes out to Kim Stephens for her hard work and dedication to publishing my other bodies of work.
Sunshine Blackrose Publication and Aliscia Melton-Hurdle a special thank you to you too for your dedication and hard work in getting this project done.

Thanking the Most High for All Blessings

Love

Nima Shiningstar-EL

Nima Shiningstar-El

About the Author

If you or someone you know is experiencing Domestic Violence please safely call The Domestic Violence Hotline at

1-866-723-3014

A Withered Rose Still Blooms

In the City of Brotherly Love and Sisterly affection...Nima Shiningstar-EL knew that she was no ordinary child. Being a young child and being bullied in school she had to sometimes create alternate worlds. Her imagination and creative way of thinking often sent her to another place and time. Throughout this journey of her mind she has created a number of works based on fiction and non-fictional situations and circumstances. It is up to you... the reader to decide and only a very few to know the sometimes horrific stories trapped between the pages of her books.

While most are asleep she takes advantage of the night with her brush against a canvas...her lens against a subject...or her pen against the paper. With all of her works poetry is always at the forefront. Her pen will continue to help build her legacy for her children and generations to come.

You can find her on Social media @nima_el/ig
Nima Shiningstar-EL /Fb

Nima Shiningstar-El

Check out these books by Nima Shiningstar-EL

Poems, Quotes & Thoughts Provoked, Nov 2014

If you or someone you know is experiencing Domestic Violence please safely call The Domestic Violence Hotline at

1-866-723-3014

A Withered Rose Still Blooms

Nima's Nights, May 2015

The Color of my Skin: This Black Woman's Poetry, March 2016

Penetrating Pieces: On Tip of My Tongue, November 2016

Nima's Nightmares: With A Twisted Mind, January 2018
(Collaboration with IshDA Godd)

Pillow Talk: What She is Thinking But May Never Say, March 2018

Nima Shiningstar-El

If you or someone you know is experiencing Domestic Violence please safely call The Domestic Violence Hotline at

1-866-723-3014

A Withered Rose Still Blooms

www.ingramcontent.com/pod-product-compliance
Lightning Source LLC
Chambersburg PA
CBHW052106070526
44584CB00017B/2353